The Thoughts of a
Completely Ordinary Teenager

C SPECTRUM

The Thoughts of a
Completely Ordinary Teenager

Born to Live

I was born a human
What does that mean
What does it make me

I was born with legs
But with no knowledge how to walk
We see and learn

I was born with a heart
A heart made of love
Not made for hate

I was born with a soul
A soul that one day will be broken

I was not born with a knowledge of how to live
Not why

Just that I should live
But how?

Table of context

Read this before you begin

Before you start reading this book, I want to tell you that some of the notes and stories might make you feel a lot of emotions, depending on what you have experienced in your life. So, think carefully before you read. Maybe it is a good idea to read with someone you trust. That way, you can talk about your thoughts as you go through the book.

You make the choice, yet I wanted to mention this since I suspect many share similar feelings. It is therefore beneficial to discuss these topics rather than holding them in and believing you are all alone. This book can tell what teenagers have on their minds during the time they grow into adults with higher responsibilities and a better understanding of how the world really works.

Keep in mind, we are all in this together - so grab a loyal person to talk and discuss your feelings with after this book.

Preface

Writing has been my form of therapy for an extended period. I have hesitated to share my feelings due to the fear of judgment. However, within the pages of this book, a collection of an "ordinary teenager's" thoughts, you might find solace and connection. My hope is that reading this will help you feel less isolated and encourage you to open up about your own thoughts. We all have thoughts we are hesitant to express, yet discussing them often relieves the burdens on our hearts and minds, even if it doesn't seem so initially.

Through this book, my objective is to help at least one individual with their inner reflections. If I can achieve that I will have positively impacted a life, fulfilling my greatest wish. Moreover, you will discover moments of self-analysis that can contribute to your health and personal growth.

I acknowledge that this topic isn't exclusive to me, yet if we collectively amplify the conversation and burst the bubble we stand to achieve substantial societal progress and personal growth.

Contained within these pages is a collection of notes I have written over the span of five years, a collection of thoughts I found difficult to share verbally. Starting from the age of 13, every note has been gradually collected.

All of us look for ways to understand things better. We want something that can give us answers that most people might not know. For some, this source might be a faith, a network of friends or family with established guidelines that is offering comfort in the face of life's uncertainties. Yet, following other people's choices without questioning for a long time isn't practical or sustainable. Each person has their own distinct life, perspective, and way of thinking especially in different situations.

The structure of this book unfolds in a manner where you will encounter the notes I've written in the first section, followed by periods of reflection and questions.

Upon concluding this journey, my hope is for you to attain a deeper understanding of both your own and others' thoughts.

My story

During the phase when my breasts were growing, my greatest desire was to have smaller breasts. However, a particular viewpoint emerged: one person believed that having larger breasts was a gift, arguing that they improved one's overall appearance. Those perspectives led me to view this as a favorable genetic trait, which allowed me to move on from such thoughts. I learned that I am perfect as I am although the "social standards" change all the time.

If you were to ask my 10-year-old self what I admire most about myself, I would've undoubtedly pointed out my freckles. These charming specks became a part of my identity and filled me with a strong sense of pride. However, at some point, a troubling thought emerged: could these freckles actually be a cause of someones' insecurity?

How could anyone perceive them as undesirable? This newfound doubt cast a shadow on something that had never posed a concern before.

Strangely, this insecurity wasn't even directly aimed at me, but it triggered an unsettling waterfall of thoughts—a case a 10-year-old should never bear.

Despite this, my determination persevered and I carried on embracing my freckles, possibly with an even greater appreciation. I came to understand that these freckles also were integral to my identity, forming an essential part of who I am just as my breasts and the rest of me.

Initially, that mindset served me well, until someone introduced a new layer of insecurity: "Perhaps you shouldn't be so thin? People might find you more appealing if you weren't comparable with a lamp-post or a pine tree". Consequently, my focus shifted to questioning my entire physique. However, facing this challenge was more unsettling compared to the experience of dealing with my freckles. I already had certain insecurity related to my body, and it didn't elicit the same positive feelings within me as my affection for my freckles did.

With the weight of another's words, I began to regard potential "solutions". However, I encountered a difficulty—my knowledge was limited to just knowing how to lose weight, not gaining it. Weight loss was the sole topic I had been educated on in the society I grew up in. As a result, I hesitated to take action because of the society's norms we have grown up with.

As I continued to age, a cascade of thoughts flooded my mind. Was I satisfied with who I had become? How could I find happiness? Was this the path I truly desired? Had I just become a reflection of the societies neverending changing norms? During a span of two years, I struggled with these questions and eventually reached a conclusion: I needed to change, again, and find myself in order to find happiness. So, I began a journey of transformation.

I chopped my hair, experimented with colors and started engaging in workouts alone in my room, away from anyone's watchful gaze. Despite my efforts, I discovered that my happiness continued to slip away from me. How could this be? I had changed my appearance; wasn't this supposed to make things better?

I thought deeply about myself, and eventually, I realized that gaining a little weight could make me feel happier. This time, it wasn't about heeding someone else's advice; it was about my personal journey. I began to read and educate myself on healthy weight gain techniques. I resolved to incorporate high-calorie foods into my diet while at the same time engaging in workouts. The aim was to build a stronger physique and, with luck, a more strong mindset.

That actually worked quite well. I began gaining weight, slowly. The results weren't as quick and big as I hoped, but I learned to be patient. Giving up was the last thing on my mind—I had come so far. I set a weight goal and gradually moved towards it. When I was almost there, something unexpected happened. I couldn't even eat a full bite of food due to the discomfort caused by intense stomach pains. Why is this happening now?? MY body seemed to let me down, again. Wasn't this what I wanted? Why now? But I couldn't give up. I had come so far, and turning back wasn't an option.

With this determination, I kept eating, working out, and living my "normal" life. After a few months and some visits to the doctor, things improved, though not completely. It wouldn't be as "easy" as before, and I accepted that. It was going to be a long, gradual journey, and I was ready to be patient. I had to work with what I had and, most importantly, not give up. One valuable lesson I learned on this journey was that you can't afford to lose what you have already fought so hard to build.

And remember;

You are the only person who has been through everything with you.

Me

Why do I always feel alone when I am by myself
But just want to be alone when I am with others

I always want to escape to what I am not
To who I am not
To where I am not

But why?
Why can I not be in the moment?
Maybe I can not match the moment I am in
Maybe I just do not match myself

You aim to be the best of you without knowing who
the best of you is

But why?
Why can you just not be yourself all the time?
Is that not enough?
Is that not who you aim to be?
The best of you is you, you then, right now and
forever

Thought exercise

Every individual holds their own unique beauty; the key lies in discovering, recognizing, and embracing it.

Think of 2-5 persons you look up to and adore on account of their looks and/or personalities.

Do you see it?

Not all the people you admire share identical appearances or personalities, yet you appreciate each of them uniquely, recognizing their individual qualities. Just as others have their unique traits, remember that you hold your own distinct characteristics too. Begin embracing this perspective next time you start comparing yourself with others.

You want to be someone and someone want to be someone else too

Sometimes you have to see the beauty in a person who just want to search and understand the world

I Keep Asking

I often find myself wondering; why am I engaged in this? What is the purpose behind my effort? Am I truly doing this for my own life or because other people told me to? When you can confidently answer "for myself" to that question it signifies that you are on the right path. If not, it is essential to make a change as the opportunity will not remain open forever.

Sometimes, it is crucial to assess what is lacking in your life. If there is something you can do to address it, take action. The sooner you initiate change, the sooner you will find greater happiness. Although the beginning might be challenging, you are striving for something meaningful.

A challenging start is essential, otherwise there is no driving force for change. Something you will eventually attain and look back on, wondering if you ever knew any different.

Is there something in your life that you wish to alter? This could encompass anything from the people you are surrounded by to your entire lifestyle. If you are aiming for a significant transformation, consider establishing incremental goals. Taking small steps is often more effective in achieving substantial changes than diving in headfirst. Remember, progress takes time.

Shift your focus from seeking happiness in others to finding it within yourself

I do not know

How come I never feel myself,
Especially I do not ever feel 'sexy'
Hard words but it is true

I am to numb in my soul, to awkward to feel cool, to
uncomfortable to be me
Maybe that is when my insecurity kicks in
Maybe that is why I never fit in

Relax they say then they laughed
Maybe not at me
But I do not know, do not care, do not know what to do
Maybe it was at me, maybe not
But still, it eats me

And I go back down again

I never feel myself
I do not hear my heart beating
Just the wind blowing through me

I fear my fears and I wonder why I have not got over it
Relax they say then they laughed, again

No wonder I can not feel myself
When I can not be the person I aim to be
I aim to be nothing
Because I do not know, do not care, do not know what to
do

Maybe it is my fault
Maybe it is everyone's
Maybe no ones

But I feel the pain
Pain of nothing
Empty air, empty heart
But still filled with ash
I do not hear my heart beating

I am to numb in my soul, too awkward to feel
cool, too uncomfortable to be me
Maybe that is when I get detached
Maybe that is why I do not fit in

And I go back down again

Bigger Perspective

You have to think about the bigger picture, even if it can be too abstract sometimes. What will the consequences of my actions have on the future? While it is essential to live in the present, contemplate this notion: What are your personal aspirations, and what steps can you take to realize them? Believe me, don't procrastinate too much. Delaying your dreams will only push them further away, obviously. So, dedicate yourself to your studies, including English, even if it isn't your strongest subject, do that one thing you have proposed, even though it is scary. Study for the person you aspire to become, rather than the occupation you wish to pursue.

What is something you consistently postponed but acknowledge the need to improve upon in the future? What tends to draw your attention away from it? How do you plan to set it in motion?

Target Image

What do you imagine for yourself when you are 80 years old? Create a clear picture of what you want to achieve or experience by that age, and then put the representative pictures in a document or a poster. It could be anything from skydiving to reaching certain job goals, or keeping the friends you want to have around.

This could also be a good opportunity to think about what boosts your energy or what just takes energy in your life. Make adjustments and focus on things that energize you or lead you toward your future goal image.

Do you care or do you just want my company?

Reflections of Life

When I began to truly think, a realization struck me: this is MY life, and I have the power to shape it. If we are so cautious that we don't truly live, if we avoid taking risks, learning from them and moving forward, what is the purpose of life? Let's instead create a life worth <u>living</u>.

I often wonder why I am here, why I exist. I have a body with arms and hands for gestures, for battling through challenges. I have legs to support me in my lowest moments and lift me in my happiest. I have lungs to breathe and a heart that may face challenges but will also experience true joy. There is a me, an entire being within me. I live, and I have myself, only me, through all the experiences I will ever encounter. So, take care of yourself and live a life worth <u>living</u>, one worth fighting for. It is hard to grasp that I exist, that there is a me, I, myself. I possess life, a body to navigate it, a brain for making decisions, both wise and opposite, and a heart for loving, hating, and forgiving.

Ask yourself, what do YOU want?

Reflect on your own desires.

Realization;

I searched for me but I searched in the wrong place, I searched for me in someone else

The Power to Change

I was alone and felt left out, like no one wanted to include me or be with me. I was a ghost. Now that I have grown older and learned from my experiences I always try to make an effort, even if it doesn't always work out as I ment, to ensure no one else goes through what I went through.

I am more attentive and approach people who are sitting alone, invite them in, or simply start a conversation. I share my chocolate with my sibling because I know how much I would have appreciated it if I were in their shoes. I let my friends go together when we are an odd number so that I am the one who ends up alone instead of someone else. But sometimes, you also have to think of yourself. However, it is challenging when you have lived like this for so many years, almost like a ghost, as a second choice to be with.

I want to know and feel that people are getting prioritized and loved for who they are. So please, next time, think about how you would want it to be if you were in the other person's shoes and then do your best. Sometimes it goes better than other times, and sometimes it might not work at all.

42

We can not decide who we were, but we can decide who we are

I have Learned

I have experienced both sides of many situations. There were times when I felt left out and invisible. I started using TikTok and my videos gained quite a few views. At first I thought "Finally, I am being noticed. I am not invisible anymore." Some of my friends believed that I just craved attention and used the app for views. Maybe I did when I felt invisible, but not now when I have realized that I am not. I often prove myself wrong but like many others, I seek confirmation in some way. If you don't get it from those around you, you will try to find it elsewhere. I am still learning every day, week, month, and year.

I have learned that some people use your vulnerabilities to make themselves feel stronger and in control. I forgive and forgive until there is nothing left to forgive because they haven't given anything in return. So, I started to become a bit more guarded and might sound tough. I tried to blend the good and the bad, hoping it would be mostly good.

I realized that the world isn't as simple as books and films make it seem. People often treat you based on their perception of you, not who you truly are, and it is influenced by their background. We should be cautious in how we treat others because we don't know their struggles, and they don't know ours.

People should discuss their relationship with themselves, but not excessively because that is seen as selfish and frowned upon. We're told to go out and save the world, save animals and our planet. But how can I save others when I can barely save myself? How can we love ourselves when we're criticized for doing things that make us feel loved? Self-love is sometimes mistaken for selfishness. Things you can view negatively can be their form of self-expression. It isn't always about hiding. Do things because you enjoy them, not because you feel obligated to.

What is something you have learned that has settled down in the back of your head?

Do you hide something inside?

Stop care about people, except for the people you CARE about.

Think about it;

You only value a message from someone you really care about, most of all via yourself. All the others are unimportant. So why do you value strangers' thoughts about you when the really valuable ones come from yourself and people who know you?

(This mindset doesn't work for everyone yet it should)

Vacuum

When you hear the word "vacuum," what is the first thing that comes to your mind?

You might think of space, where you are free from gravity and floating without control. It is similar to the feeling of being trapped, being powerless in your own life, which is hard to put into words. "Vacuum" is the closest term I could find to describe it and it is tough to grasp unless you've experienced something similar.

It can also implement the feeling of living on autopilot, of not controlling your life, just going on without reflecting on what is going on around you. The best way to explain it is through the analogy of space, where you have no control and feel nothing. I felt completely empty.

In a short time, I found myself in this state, which we can call "Space-syndrome." It robs you of control, leaving you staring blankly and unable to influence anything. You experience a mix of emotions but it is mostly just emptiness, like how gravity affects people in space – the circumstances around my life had a profound impact on me.

In that time I could also describe it as being underground or more like being underwater or as if there were sound reductions in the world around myself that blocked life from me - you are just not there. Your body may be in the room but never your soul, thoughts or sense. What causes this feeling? How does it arise in the first place and how can you come out from this bubble of vacuum?

I don't have the answer to that - only you do by asking yourself why you may be feeling this all the way until you reach and can identify the root of the problem.

Who am I

Staring, staring, staring

Into the life

The life that passes by

The life I had, the life I have, the life I am going to live

Staring, staring, staring

To the sky all blue

Without stars, I can still see the moon

The moon and the sun together that soon will explode

The moon with its gravity

The sun with its warmth

Staring, staring, staring

To the person I aim to be

To me

Who am I

Staring through my soul but see nothing

Nothing between, under or over

With nothing inside I live my days

Staring, staring, staring

To the moon, the sun and the life I could have

Staring to the point where I am all zoned out

Feelings zoned, everything is out of reach

Staring, staring, staring into the life that has passed by

Phones
The Distraction of Life

What's scary is that regardless of what you say, do or how you act, it is always stronger.

Everyone seems so interested in each other's lives online but when you are with someone in real life, you don't really care about what they're saying. Even when you are on vacation or similar outings you still spend a lot of time on your phone. You check out what others are doing and where they are right now instead of enjoying your own experiences.

I am so tired of pretending, pretending that this isn't a problem. I see it, and most frightening is that I am a part of it. Everyone needs to wake up and look around because it is what I've been doing and I am starting to get scared. No one is perfect and no one will ever be. The least everyone can do no matter who you are is to try, try to understand their actions and the consequences of them. Especially when it comes to using mobile phones or other digital tools.

I have understood for a long time that it has been a significant issue but now when I have seen it with my own eyes, I've felt so bad that I have to change this and do something about it. That is why I am writing this little note, hoping that more people wake up, try to understand and improve their behavior and actions. Everyone knows about it, but far too few do anything about it.

Since mobile phones came along, more and more people have fallen into depression and anxiety and I've wondered why for a long time. So, one day, I decided to "research" and investigate it a bit more. I looked around to observe people and their behavior with mobile phones. I didn't get far before I saw that everyone on the bus was glued to their phones, completely silent and no one was talking to each other. The same during school breaks. Before the children played on the playground, the playground is now replaced with a technical device with everyone's lives on it. Same with parenting. I saw parents being engrossed in their phones instead of being with their children and so on.

What does your phone give you?

Society

Someone said some things to you that you went home and thought of, maybe even overthought. The person who spoke those words to you might be doing the same, lying down and overanalyzing what they said. The next day, both of you avoid each other because of the nerves between you. This is why it is crucial to talk about it. If they weren't overthinking, you should still have a conversation with them. After all, if they don't know what they did wrong, how can they ever change and improve?

It might sound like a challenging mission, but you need to shift your perspective. Try it for a day; view everything as possible and stay positive. Forget the negativity and be your authentic self. See who sticks around; perhaps they'll perceive you differently. Did people treat you differently? Was it strange?

Consider how you'd like to be treated if you were in their shoes. If you switched roles, do you appreciate how "you" are behaving?

Society

I understand that I am not the first to write about these matters but everyone has a unique viewpoint and I wanted to share mine. Hopefully, you've learned something from my mistakes because that is what this book is all about: learning from your own mistakes. But before you make those mistakes, look around. Can you learn from others' mistakes? Did you appreciate how someone treated you or spoke to you that day?

Everyone is different, but try to treat people the way you'd like to be treated. Share food, cake, or appreciation - the things people didn't share with you, with someone else. Assist others so they don't end up where you've been, and do it with respect.

Take care of yourself.

Everyone has their own story

What is yours?

How has society affected you?

Think of or write down five things when the society has affected you

You should live <u>your</u> life, not survive it. But sometimes you have to survive in order to live

Proudbook

In late May 2021, I started to write more. It wasn't necessarily because I had a deep love for writing, however it was driven by a growing self-doubt that seemed to accelerate with each passing day. I found myself questioning every word I spoke, every action I took and how I presented myself. All I could see was the negative side of things. I thought of what I could have done differently or better, constantly rethinking my choices. Every comment and word felt as it slipped out of my mouth in the wrong way. I felt like a complete failure in every aspect of my life and everything seemed to be bizarre and strange.

Nevertheless, what actually occurred in May of 2021 was a turning point. I began to wake up and understand my own actions and behavior. I had a sudden urge to change for the better. So, I made a commitment to myself: I would write down at least one good thing I did every day, yes, you read that correctly, every. single. day.

I would focus on the positive actions I had taken, regardless of their size and appreciate them. I was willing to face my own challenges and discover the goodness that I had been blind to before.

The next text, "History", will delve into the day I wrote the first entry in my "proudbook" and the thoughts that inspired it. It also serves as an inspiration for you to carry with you in your own reflections.

Sometimes I feel like it is not me that is moving my body, it is someone else. May be the society, may be a feeling. But I do not know because I have no control.

History

Little happenings can lead to big changes

I began writing on May 27 2021, the same day as my oral "national exam" in Spanish. It is important to note that I didn't particularly love working with languages. I wasn't a fast learner when it came to languages, but I refused to give up easily. There was still a flicker of fighting spirit left in me. I did what I could and was accepting that I couldn't do more.

The unique thing about that day was the extreme nervousness. I felt a level of anxiety I had never experienced before. My Spanish classes over the past three years had been quite challenging for me. We had a change in teachers every year, and my brain struggled to grasp the finer details we were taught. Learning took a lot of effort and time. The classes were often chaotic. During the first year, some of my classmates didn't respect our teacher.

The second year felt somewhat wasted because it seemed like I hadn't learned much at all. It was during the third and final year that we finally got a "real" teacher who had respect for both herself and her students. The classes became less chaotic and I finally felt like I could concentrate and learn more.

In the first two years, I achieved the highest score in all the Spanish classes, even though I knew I wasn't at that level. My knowledge was weak and I told myself that I should aim for a middle score at the end of my last course. My first score in the final course was a middle score, which was the score I believed I deserved all along. I wasn't disappointed, on the contrary I felt proud that I had achieved my goal and had a teacher who was fair in grading and teaching. However, maintaining that middle score required a lot from me.

With the stress of all the other final exams in the other 16 subjects, the day of the oral national Spanish exam arrived. I had high expectations for myself,and my performance anxiety was at its peak. I had prepared for this day for a long long time and my heart raced with anticipation.

When the moment came, my classmate and I were called to the classroom to sit in front of our teacher and the preparation and information materials. My nervousness began to swell as I sat down, growing more intense with each passing second.

After our teacher provided instructions and gave us some time to prepare, it was time to start speaking. I was still shaking with nervousness, so I let my classmate begin. As time went on, my nervousness increased and my ability to think clearly diminished. Then it was my turn, I found myself unable to speak in any language including my own. The silence in the room, as everyone listened to me, only added to my nervousness. It felt like being in a vacuum, and I felt completely overwhelmed. My teacher could see my nervousness and gave me a minute to collect myself, but all I could think about was how my thoughts and knowledge had slipped away.

I tried my best to regain self-control, even though tears welled up in my throat, I felt like running away any minute. Nevertheless, I managed to speak a few words, and I remember trying to use as many words as possible to improve my sentences. Would this be enough for a middle score? Had I failed the LAST and crucial exam? Would all my hard work over the past three years be in vain because of this test? It couldn't happen.

Our teacher thanked us, and I left the classroom with the same nervousness that had plagued me upon entering, if not worse now. The results were supposed to be posted after the last pair had completed the exam. As the last pair walked out, my anxiety intensified. All I could do was wait, stress, breathe, and repeatedly refresh the result site. Finally, the notification arrived, but I was too anxious to open it. It was the climax of three years of effort. Had I succeeded?

The first thing I saw when I opened the site was a big number with a middle score in the center of the screen. I.had.made.it. I wanted to cry of all the overwhelming feelings. I had actually achieved it, something that had felt impossible just a few minutes earlier. Thanks to all the hard work I had put in over the past three years I didn't give up, even when it seemed impossible.

Despite the mental blackout and the anxiety I had felt during the last national exam, the exam that would control everything for me, I had proven to myself that it is worth trying even if the odds seem small. All these small achievements gathered and lead to greater results over time, more than you might realize.

This is the reason why you shouldn't give up - the small things lead to bigger changes

You can do it; you just need to want it.

The note in my proudbook:

"Today I am proud of myself because of that I achieved a middle score in my final exams and therefore in the whole complete course even though I got a black out during it"

When people dream they often come to the conclusion that "oh I can never be like THOSE people". What they forget is that "these people" also are just people. People who have stood there and probably said these exact same words and are properly still.

The Mask

"If I don't tell anyone it doesn't exist"

This thought was the reason I kept so many things inside, rather than talking about them. My reasoning was that if I didn't share certain things that were weighing me down, I could pretend that everything was as it should be and people would "treat me normally". All I wanted was to live a normal life, free from the chaos in my head. I feared that if I told everyone, I'd be left feeling exposed and unable to escape from it.

What I didn't realize at the time was that sharing with even just one person wouldn't drown me. It did the opposite, it lifted me out of the sea of my worries. This journey taught me a crucial lesson: if you want to change something, you have to change your behavior or something in your lifestyle because otherwise, it will remain the same. In my case, I needed to speak to someone about my thoughts. If I did nothing, those thoughts would remain trapped in my head. It is a part of you and you have to accept it as a part of you before you can begin to process it.

The message here is simple: try something different because if you don't, things will stay the same.

We all have a multitude of thoughts, some similar and others quite unique. Here is a space for you to reflect on your thoughts. Perhaps even to process and understand them. But first, I'll share a few of my thoughts, and maybe you will find some familiarity in them.

Many of our thoughts are similar, just painted differently due to the various actions and processes that give rise to them. Remember, it is a part of you and you have to accept it as a part of you before you can turn to process it.

Answers (in my head) to the question: "Why do you not open up to someone?"

1. "I Felt that If I didn't say something I could pretend that everything was "normal" (what that even means) and that was everything I wanted. Because if no one knew about it, I would be treated as usual and that realization made it possible for me to get away from these thoughts".

2. "I have listened so much to everybody else about their thoughts so I didn't want to intrude and talk about me and my thoughts, they already have so much in their head to think about. I would just make it worse".

3. "I am scared that they are just talking it over with their problems and thoughts, that I wouldn't get it all out of my head when I start. I hate when that happens, especially when you are not a person that opens up a lot. When you finally do, you want someone who listens to YOU, not take it over to them instead and make you and your thoughts seem smaller".

Why I stopped speak up for myself

Every time I speak up or get annoyed people start laughing at me since they think I am "cute" or whatever when I am upset, they never seem to take me seriously. No one takes me seriously and I can't take the humiliation to be laughed at so it is better to be quiet. Everything I want is to be taken seriously as the person I am, to be accepted, to be someone in the room instead of someone's shadow.

Today I am free, free from the thought I never thought I would be free from

💭

Thoughts Through Quotes

Life

Isn't a guarantee

So do what you want to do while you still have the change

Don't make those easy excuses

You will regret it

When you one day have pushed your dreams to far

If someone really likes you, they like YOU. Just you. not the person you try and want to be in your head.

No one can never be .just. like. you.
because you are the perfect version of you

The only person you have to manifest is yourself, because if you change yourself for somebody else's words you are going to make a mistake. If they leave you, you realize that you do not have yourself left

They have taken "you" away from you when they left

You are going to be with yourself all your life so it is time to get to know you and spend more time loving yourself

They are insecure about their body, their smile, their walk, they are insecure about everything, but what should they think when no one tells them that they are ugly, or pretty? When no one talks to them at all?

No wonder why they is so insecure

They like people who are confident, but why are you not trying to be confident too so you can like you too?

Think of all you have been through, <u>you</u> did it. You made it through it then, so then you can do it now, tomorrow and forever

The ONLY way you can change something in the past is to change your upcoming future

Your shape does not matter and here is why

Do you ever think when you open a gift:
"ew what an ugly shape"

No, you open it up and see what's on the
inside. Some presents are more difficult to
open than others, but it still can be opened.
Just like you and your heart.

We don't see people's real struggles, just the frame they try to express out to others

Chasing

I keep going, going, going up, but I still fall.

I am going going going to do great, but not just now

Because I am falling falling falling apart into
thousand of billions of hearts

And I keep running running running, but for what?

I am just giving up

But I am keeping firm for a future that I do not know
exists

My future that always is far away; it is never here it is
always there - in the future

Something that makes me feel alive

I want something that makes me feel alive.
Something, a feeling, a sense of yearning, that makes
me shiver

I want something that can turn my inside, smile and
childless out, my happiness lies inside of me yet to
deep down for me to dig

I strive to dig deeper to find my something, a feeling,
a sense of something, a sense of feeling alive

Ending

As I wrap up this journey, I hope the words in these pages have made you feel a connection or helped you think about your thoughts and feelings in a new way. Writing has been my way of dealing with thoughts and feelings and it wasn't easy to share them. I was afraid people would judge me, but my goal was always to help others see that we all have thoughts we are uncertain to express.

We all carry these thoughts, worried that they might burden others or make us seem different. But by sharing them, we can find common ground and feel less alone in our struggles. It is a reminder that we are all humans dealing with our own inner battles.

I never meant to claim that my experiences were unique. We all face the challenge of understanding ourselves and our place in the world. My hope was to add my voice to the conversation and encourage personal growth and understanding.

In these pages, you have explored my thoughts and reflections and I hope they have given you something to think about in your own life.

In the end, if this book has offered even a little insight or helped one person on their journey of self-discovery, then it has done its job. Our lives are all different but when we listen to each other and share our thoughts, we can create a bigger understanding that goes beyond our individual perspectives.

As you finish reading, keep exploring your own thoughts and the thoughts of others. It is through this exploration that we keep learning and growing.

You are not alone, talk and you will see

And remember;

These aren't established facts. They are just thoughts. Thoughts of a Completely Ordinary Teenager.

At least I lived before I died

Publisher: BoD · Books on Demand, Stockholm, Sweden
Print: Libri Plureos GmbH, Hamburg, Germany
ISBN: 978-91-8080-025-9